# BHAGAVAD GITA

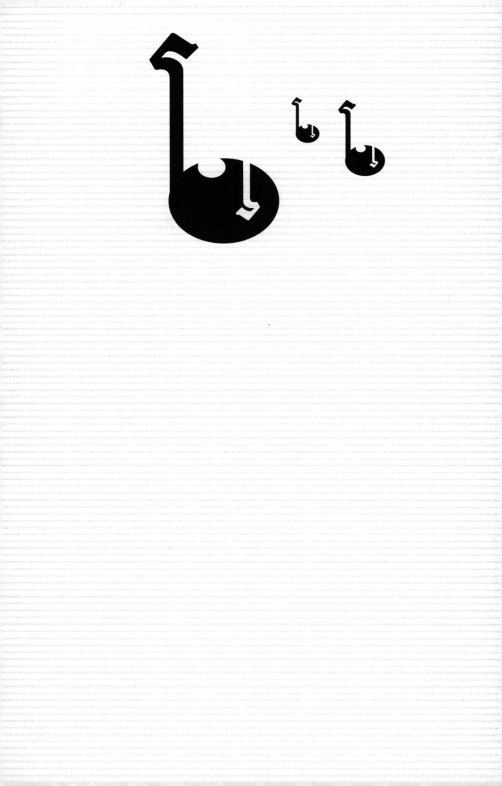

# BHAGAVAD GITA

## a translation of the poem

By Mani Rao

91st Meridian Books

ÆB

Autumn Hill Books
Iowa City, Iowa

**a leaf
a page**

# TRANSLATOR'S NOTE

The *Gita* is a poem, and in Sanskrit, chanted or read aloud. The stanzas of the *Gita* do not have end-rhymes but have internal symmetry including assonant word-pairs. Plain prose translations cannot convey this liveliness. Metrical translations have a more basic challenge—fidelity to meaning. Between prosaic prose translations and straitjacketed metrical translations is the territory of free verse. However, most translations into free verse focus on line breaks. They look like poetry, but do not sound like poetry, and do not attempt to catch the language-play of the Sanskrit *Gita*. Whether prose or poetry, whether by the letter or by the spirit, translations have adhered to the stanza structure.

Studying previous translations, I could not help but feel that the *Gita's* status as a holy text has held back the translator's hand, making it hesitant to delete even a rhetorical space-filler such as "indeed," or to shift the order of lines within a stanza. Word-for-word and line-for-line translations create obscurities and retard the pace of communication in English. Available correspondences for the *Gita's* pivotal concepts such as *brahman*, *ātman*, and *karma*, prove uncommunicative. *Ātman*, for example, is regularly translated as soul or self. Soul is a safe, familiar word, but vague, for we do not know what exactly it refers to, and self is a concept understood in different ways. Sometimes Krishna is referring to you, and sometimes to the ungendered, immortal, indestructible it, who you really, really are. When Matthew Arnold and Juan Mascaro consistently translate *ātman* as soul, they arrive at the idea of how to purify the soul in 6.12, which goes against the grain of the *Gita's* teaching about the always-pure state of the *ātman*. No wonder then that *Gita* translations tend to be accompanied by footnotes and commentary; the reader has to be studious to penetrate the translation. It is also why commentaries prove useful: they achieve communication and integrate subtext and context into the text in a way that word-for-word translations cannot access; however, they take us further away from the poem. My method addresses this gap in the tradition of *Gita* translations. I follow the order of the text, but take the cognitive unit variably as it occurs at each instance in the *Gita*—in the line, stanza, or even across a group of stanzas. My lineation style fits the interchangeable word order of Sanskrit syntax. It helps me convey several points at once, present the text in different directions (see 10.08), and keep track of different narrative threads spatially.

I delete nothing except what I regard as overly rhetorical or repetitious. I omit the first ten verses in the second chapter because it recapitulates the first chapter and retards the pace—but every verse is numbered to help the reader who chooses to study the details. I do not omit any word that conveys a philosophical point; I may ignore *maharatha*, for instance, which often seems like a metrical filler, but not *avyayam*, although it comes up suspiciously often. When I comment on (rather than explain) a point, or add a word to link and interpret ideas, I use parentheses. I italicize and explain terms the first time they occur, after which I treat them as a part of the vocabulary. I consider explanation of new terms and concepts imperative; Arjuna's learning depends on understanding what Krishna says, and the reader's learning depends on understanding the translation.

My choices sometimes rely on etymology to bring into play the resonance of the word in Sanskrit: for example, *sat* (truth) comes from the root "to be," or what is—so truth is what is, and untruth is what isn't. The process also works the other way, into English; thus, *dhyana* translates as "meditate" and *samadhi*, as "trans meditate." Familiar phrases and idiomatic expressions are vibrant modes to help resituate the text in a place where the reader can more easily connect to Krishna. In 10.21–10.32, with lists of Hindu deities, I think the specifics will weaken the impact of the concept, so I stack the comparison, and if the reader knows what "sun" is to "lights," s/he can apply that concept to the next line, "marichi among maruts." I have not translated epithets for Arjuna and Krishna except when there is an overt logic to their use. As Arjuna, I address Krishna as Krishna, until the revelation in Chapter 11, when I find myself addressing Krishna as God. Krishna uses the masculine pronoun to connect with Arjuna, but Arjuna is a proxy for the reader — in this translation, the addressee becomes s/he, and via myself, becomes "herself."

Stanzas that depart radically from the surface meaning of the original occur when a literal translation would be uncommunicative, and when the emotive moment calls for a deeper reading. 1.1 is such an instance. Translated literally: *In the field of righteousness, in the field of kuru, gathered, eager to fight—my sons, and Pandu's sons, indeed, what did they do, Sanjaya? Dharma* can be translated as righteousness, virtue, truth, duty. *Kshetra* as field, region.

*Dharmakshetre*, in translatese, is "in the field of righteousness," and all the gravitas of the Sanskrit word, and the import of the scene, is lost in the repetitious habit and history of literal translation. When I let *kshetra* speak to me, I gather: in the area of, in the realm of, in matters of, at, of, context. Dhrtarashtra's question equates *dharma* and *kuru*. The physical place *kuru* is not just the scene or setting, it is larger than life, context, situation. What is the situation? The Kauravas cheated in a dice game and ousted the Pandavas, who want revenge; the Kauravas are in power, the Pandavas are in the right, and the only way to resolve the conflict is through a battle. In this verse, place and situation have converged into a point of no return. I translate this as "when it came to that," placing pressure on "that." I note the tension in *yuyutsavaha*: these warriors are keen to have it out. I have a mental image of two sides facing and about to unmask themselves. I take in the words "my sons" and "Pandu's sons" with their full weight of what has gone on in the Mahabharata up until that point: might vs. right. What did they do = who did what, what happened first/next.

dhrtrashtra to sanjaya:
and when it came to that
might   right   face-off
what  happened who
did what?

I use a somewhat different technique for verses 2.22 – 2.25, where Krishna explains "soul." The concept: you are not the body, you wear the body, you are the embodied (*dehi*, this, it). To translate *dehi*, I avoid the usual equivalents *self* and *soul*, and rely on *you*, allowing its implications to open up along with the text.

(literally)
*Just as, having cast away worn-out garments*
*A man takes new ones*
*Thus, having cast away worn out bodies*
*The embodied meets/joins other new ones (bodies)*  2.22

My translation collapses this into two lines. I emphasize *you*, and summarize the point in a line. I also imitate the vedantic idea of *neti* ("not this"), i.e., how discarding reveals the true you. I stack the analogy.

you discard old clothes for the new
you discard one worn-out body for another
you are not your body

In 2.23 there is more information about how the *dehi* is invulnerable.

(literally)
*Weapons pierce not this*
*Fire burns not this*
*Waters wet not this*
*Wind withers not this* 2.23

The first three lines of 2.24 repeat the content but shift the focus to the *dehi*.

(literally)
*Not-to-be-pierced, this*
*Not-to-be-burned, this*
*Not-to-be-wetted, this; Not to be withered, this*
*Eternal, Everywhere-going, Fixed*
*Unmoving, this, primordial* 2.24

I fuse 2.23 and 2.24.

| weapons | cannot pierce | \| this \| | unpiercable |
| fire | burn | \| who \| | unburnable |
| water | wet | \| you \| | unwettable |
| wind | dry | \| really \| | undryable |
| | | \| are \| | |

forever
            free
      fixed
            fromever

The pairs in the last two lines that resonate with each other, are *nityah* and *sanatanah* (eternal, and primordial / ancient / old — time stretching into the past eternal and the future eternal) and *sarvagatah* and *sthanuh* (going everywhere, and fixed). I let these pairs work together. The first set becomes "forever" and "fromever." The next set is absurd in English, for how anything could go everywhere and yet be fixed? The word points to *freedom*, I translate this as "free."

Lines 3 and 4 of 2.24 present some unfathomable concepts about the embodied, and so it is time for 2.25 to explain why.

Literally:
*Un-apparent/manifest this, unthinkable this*
*Unchanging this, it is said*
*Therefore having known this*
*Not to mourn you're worthy of* 2.25

Line 4 of this stanza repeats as line 4 of 2.26. This is emphatic, and from it I take as central the contrast between the unfathomable "embodied," and the limitations of a confused Arjuna. What is reported about the "embodied" is beyond Arjuna; he cannot *grasp* the idea. I convert the "un-manifest" and "un-thinkable" into the tools of apprehension — senses and thoughts.

2.25            can not be felt by the senses
                can not be grasped by thought

                beyond the variable

I do so because the next stanza, 2.26, goes further into "thought"— no matter what you choose to think about the embodied, anyway, you must not mourn. The repetition of line 4 in 2.25 and 2.26 insists that you do not deserve to—you are not worthy of—mourning the "embodied." The stanza puts Arjuna in his place. When you know that the embodied cannot be seen/felt or thought of, you are in no position to mourn for it, and it is not for you to mourn.

understand it
 is not for you to mourn

A strategy so varied within itself and from previous translations is only possible *because* of previous translations, because of the learning of tradition, with interpretive possibilities and bewilderment nicely documented. Previous perspectives, both translations and commentaries, form the thickly layered palimpsest of the *Gita* tradition that one can, and must, rely on. I refer to, and am grateful to, Sankara's *Gita-Bhasya*, the translations of C. Zaehner, Barbara Stoller, Graham Schweig, Juan Mascaro, Prabhavananda-Isherwood, Matthew Arnold, P. Lal, and commentaries by Swami Bhaktivedanta and Swami Chinmayananda, Winthorp Sargeant (who, in turn, refers to Ramanuja for interpretive notes), and Bhagawan Sathya Sai Baba's discourses. And yet, when on occasion, I have had trouble fathoming a stanza or line, despite — as well as because of — turning to various commentaries, I was helped by recordings of the *Gita*: I found the recording by Swami Brahmananda especially expressive and clarifying.

I must confess I never imagined I would care to engage in an intimate and enduring conversation with a text that spells out birth-caste as *karmic*, or killing as *dharmic*. I took consolation in the wider narrative that is not as much about fighting as about detachment — Krishna recommends the *sattvic* path as the most joyous, and non-violence is part of the *sattvic* path; whereas, Arjuna, as a warrior, is a *rajasic* doer. Besides, the battle is within the clan, the challenge is about standing up for what one believes is "right," about readiness *even* to oppose one's own kin. Thus, the *Gita's* recommendation is to take a broader view of humanity, and be genuinely impartial. As for caste, I temper my objections with the point Krishna repeatedly makes, that all beings are part of the divine. As I read and re-read the *Gita*, it is Krishna's admission of love for the devotee that most moved me. Translators tend to present *bhajami* as *I serve* or *I worship* when it refers to devotees, and as *I reward* when it refers to Krishna (see 4.11); my sense of Krishna's feelings towards the devotee guides me not to differentiate between the two instances. How can Krishna possibly not be in service to the devotee, when he plays the role of Arjuna's driver in the story, and takes the time (over seven hundred stanzas) to enlighten Arjuna? Time and time again in the *Gita*, Krishna declares love for the devotee, and seems to long for the devotee's wisdom and love. The *Gita* is not only a poem, it is a love poem. May fidelity, then, be deep, complex, and lively.

An army of friends participated in my experience of the *Gita* and this translation — I only acknowledge here those who were in the thick of it. My father was my first reader: he read every chapter as I drafted it, and his responsiveness vindicated my translation strategy. My mother's sense of humor renewed my energy and kept me grounded — memorably, when

I expressed nervousness about confronting the revelation or *visvarupam* in Chapter 11, she said, "Relax, it's just a lot of hands and legs." My teacher Dr. Sarasvati Mohan gave me the drill in Sanskrit lessons and pointed me to valuable references. I realized that it was the *Gita* I would translate in Professor Dr. Giuseppe Natale's class on translation theory. An expansive context of Ernest Fenollosa, Henri Michaux, David Slavitt, Marte Werner & c. arrived with translator and poet, Professor Donald Revell. Among numerous Iowa friends who enabled this translation's journey, some have been more directly connected with the publication of this book: the International Writing Program opened doors to community, editors of *eXchanges* conjured a timely journal debut, and Autumn Hill Books and *91ˢᵗ Meridian* booked it.

1.01    dhrtrashtra to sanjaya:
            & when it came to that
            might    right    face-off
            what happened  who
            did what

1.02    duryodhana took in the
        enemy line up & said
        to dronacharya:

1.03            no thanks to you prof.
                trained by you  dhrstadyumna
                chief of the other side
                has put it together

1.04-1.06       a who's who
                of heroes            each
                                     a bhim
                                     an arjun

                yuyudhana – virata – drupada –
                dhrstaketu – cekitana  – & the king of kasi  –
                purujit – kuntibhoj – bullish saibya
                yudhaamanyu – uttamaujas – abhimanyu – &
                the famous five
                sons of draupadi

1.07    not that we're less
       prepped

1.08    we've got bhishma
       & karna
       & kripacharya
       & asvatthama
       & vikarna
       & the somadatta sons
       &

1.09    all sorts of weapons
       at their fingertips
       for my sake their
       life on the line

1.10    & yet it's not
       enough
       our bhishma to
       their bhima so

1.11    in every move
       stick to your roles
       keep your head  bhishma
       safe

1.12– grandlion bhishma
 1.13 bellowed
       yeaarrghh
  & blew his

       conch erupt his
       troops took it up
       on drums & cymbals
       & trumpets

       what a riot

1.14    until

        from a sleek chariot
        on two white steeds leapt
        unearthly sound

1.15–   krishna's panchajanya &
 1.18   arjuna's devadatta

        then bhima's hungry paundra – king yudhistira's victory call – nakula's
        nice tone – sahadeva's gembloom – each

        announced himself
        unique

        king of kashi – sikhandin – dhrstadyumna – virata – unbeatable satyaki –
        drupada – his sons in law the five pandavas –
        & powerarm abhimanyu
        revved

1.19    shook earth & sky
        busted  your sons'
        hearts

1.20             armies all set
             weapons about to clash

             under the hero-hanuman banner
             arjuna reached for his bow
             & paused

        to krishna:

1.21             sir  can we go
             to a vantage point
             between armies

1.22–1.25          who's there          who's
                   to fight for evil    sweet on evil
                   duryodhana

          chariot parked
          in no man's land
          in front of bhishma & drona & all the chiefs
          arjuna said   see
          & saw

1.26–27            familiars            foster fathers & fathers' fathers & fathers
                                        in law & uncles & teachers &
                                        brothers & friends &
                                        godsons & grandsons
1.28–     & said
 1.30              pitiful

                   these people         war urgent
                   are
                   my people            i feel

                   drained              my
                   mouth's dry          my
                   tremble              is me my every
                   hair in shock        my
                   bow slips            i'm
                   feverish             i can barely
                   stand                my mind
                   wheels

1.31               all the signs are grave
                           no good can come
                           from killing my own

1.32               don't wanna be a hero
                   don't need no empire
                           what's there to enjoy
                                what's the point of it all

1.33    all those
for whom i'd want
to live it up
are here to die

1.34         fathers & fathers' fathers & fathers
in law & brothers in law &
sons & son's sons & teachers
& uncles & others

1.35    i'm not into
this      they-kill-so-i-kill

not if i was paid three
worlds   as for mere earth
           pah!

1.36    what kind of fun's
in murdering the sons
of dhrtarashtra

      the sin will do us in

1.37    dhrtarashtra's sons are
family  how can we
happily
slaughter our own

1.38    they don't know       greed won't let them
                                think
how blind it is this
fratricide

1.39    but we can see       shall we not say no
devastation
of the clan

1.40–    family = values
1.44            de structing → chaos

                when lawlessness
                = law
                        our women violated
                            "castes" mixed up
                                    rites undone
                                            ancestors let down

                that totally ruins the family
                & destroyers of the family            HELL !


2.11    krishna:
                nice speech  arjuna  but

                the truly wise
                know better

                than to be sad
                over life that's gone
                        or not

                life & death pass

2.12            i was never not
                & never won't
                be

                you too
                & them

2.13            you
                change    in this body      from child to adult & decrepit
                & you
                change    into another body  again

2.14–2.15        sensations    cold heat
                         pleasure pain
              are mortal   they come & go

stay
unruffled    by them get ready
for immortality

2.16           if it isn't      it isn't
                    true       real

what you call reality
is really virtual
                    reality

your reality's materiality

(material = changeable = mortal = untrue = immaterial)

it seems as if    but
there's no
truth in fiction

what is what    is
clear to a seer

2.17–2.18        that by which this
immaterial matter
is permeated
is permanent

bodies end
the embodied     timeless         (let's call it "it")
can not            be measured destroyed

        so fight  arjuna

2.19               s/he who thinks it kills &
                          s/he who thinks it is killed

                          don't get
                          it
                          is neither

                          it   is who you really are

2.20               never was it born
                          never will it die
                          nor ever having been will ever not be

                          forever
                          fromever
                          unchanging in the changing
                                        body

2.21               if you know you
                          are indestructible   eternal   birthless   changeless
                                      for instance
                          how can you believe you
                          are the one to kill
                          & who do you kill

2.22               you discard      old clothes for the new
                          you discard      one worn-out body for another

                          you are          not your body

| 2.23–2.24 | weapons | cannot | pierce | \| this \| | unpiercable |
|---|---|---|---|---|---|
| | fire | | burn | \| who \| | unburnable |
| | water | | wet | \| you \| | unwettable |
| | wind | | dry | \| really \| | undryable |
| | | | | \| are \| | |

forever
   free
      fixed
fromever

2.25      can not be felt by the senses
can not be grasped by thought

beyond the variable

understand it
    is not for you to mourn

2.26      even if you imagine it
birthing dying
recurring
    still not your place to mourn

2.27      it's the "born" who are guaranteed to "die"
it's the "dead" who are "reborn"
    pointless for you to mourn

2.28      & birth to death
is the obvious part
the middle part

your true beginning & end
is hidden
    so what

2.29    the truth is
so awesome that

some visualise it
some talk about it
some hear about it

all awed
none the wiser

2.30    this – it –        (some call it soul)
is indestructible in
everyone's body
            so no need to mourn

2.31    war = warrior's duty
= your duty
            fear not

2.32    happy the warriors        what luck!
to get a war like this        open heaven gates

2.33    to not do what's
right    your duty
            this war
            your glory
that's wrong

2.34    disgraceful
            people will talk
            the talk won't die
better to die

2.35    you'll be seen as a wimp among warriors
be littled among your fans

2.36    unspeakable      the way your enemies will mock you
what's more awful than that

2.37    if you die you'll get to heaven
if you live you'll enjoy yourself

get up  get
ready to fight

2.38    do the math
        happiness = sorrow
        gain = loss
then take on the war you can't lose

2.39    now all that's explained in *samkhya* samkhya philosophy

the question is  how
to practice it  how

to embrace it  to
lose karma's braces

2.40                there is a path

                    no effort's wasted
                    even a little bit of practice
                    helps you          fear less

2.41-2.42           the smart ones are singleminded
                    clear about it

                    ignoramuses
                    have endless opinions
                    give flowery speeches  &
                    swear by the veda
                    gzillion ritual pleas
                    for pleasure/power

2.43            they
           want nothing less than heaven
           get nothing more than rebirth

2.44            stuck
           distracted their
           mind can't stay still
           to trans meditate

2.45      the world      of the veda
           is made
           of qualities
           three      (i'll explain more later)

           without them be
                free
           without
           swinging      between opposites      (heat/cold
                pairs      yin/yang
                extremes      pain/pleasure)

           without playing
                the getting & keeping game

           be anchored
           in yourself      (not in the vedic rulebook)

2.46      vedic rituals
           like a well surrounded by water

           useless
           when you have
           knowledge

*Mani Rao*

2.47  (back to the path  of activity  *karma yoga*
                every action       work
                has an equal reaction   result
                    we call it "fruit of action")

you've got to do what you've got to do
not get hung up on the outcome

work for work's sake
have no agenda

which doesn't mean you
sulk from the world
action

2.48  steady          do what must be done
                without differences
      be the same     undifferent
            in success
            in failure

practice level headedness
level headedness = proof of practice

2.49  so much for karma yoga    good
      but the thinker's path
      even better

rely on reason
& you'll understand     what makes the agenda-seeker so
                wretched

13

2.50           think about it
                   drop the notion
                   of "good" & "bad" actions

                   get a fix on yoga

                   skill means
                   anything done well

2.51           the wise let go
                          of fruit of action
                   & they're let go
                          from the birthdecay chain
                          (aka reincarnation or transmigration)

2.52           when your wisdom cuts through delusion
                   you won't care for the official revelations

2.53           transcending scriptures when you
                   transcend in meditation totally still

                   you'll get there
                          the ultimate        yoga
                   united
                          with it who you really are

2.54    arjuna:
                   this wise 'n steady type
                          who can deep meditate

                   what's s/he like  how does s/he
                        walk  talk  sit

2.55    krishna:         s/he
                  ignores desires
                           they come & go

                           with self
                  is happy to simply be

2.56              in bad times not down
                           in good times not up

                  passion  fear  anger
                           etcetera gone

2.57              in everything wants
                           nothing

                  pleasant & unpleasant's alike

                  neither salutes nor dislikes

2.58              can disengage sense organs from sensuous things  completely
                  as a tortoise withdraws into shell its limbs

2.59              when you don't feed on them
                  temptations drop off

                  it takes more time to
                  lose the taste
                  for pleasure

                  but after the ultimate experience
                           liberation

                  that too is a non issue

2.60              wild      the senses run
                           away with the
                  earnest seeker mind

2.61         so the wise 'n steady has
senses under control
sits in deep thought of me

2.62         instead of meditating on me if you
meditate on indulgences you

feel fond
& then you want

then frustrated
fury

2.63         fury clouds
sends memory for a spin
intelligence for a toss
       you'll be lost

2.64         the self controlled has no
likes & dislikes

can be mobbed by temptations
& be serene

2.65         & in this serene
     sorrows vanish
     mind steadies

2.66                by contrast the
undisciplined seeker has
no understanding no focus no peace
     so no happiness

2.67                when mind chases senses
understanding's swept away

windtossed ship

2.68      (summary)
the wise 'n steady =
s/he who has self-control
withdraws senses from temptations

2.69      the difference    (between her & others)
     day & night
          a different world

s/he's awake    you're asleep
her truth light   you can't see

     & vice versa

for the seer
your world means zilch

2.70      s/he's oceanlike   exposed to desire rivers
                    any which way
                    yet
steadydeep
peace full

2.71      s/he has dropped all   "i want"
                         "me" "my"
                         egoism
goes freely
in peace

2.72      this is it

once here    never fooled again
stays here   right to the end

then bliss blown
uberliberation   *brahman* = ultimate = capital g o d
brahmanirvana  (different from the small gods  deities)

3.01    arjuna:

        if the life of the mind   thought  is
        better than the life of
        activity

        why drive me
        to gory acts

3.02

        your mixed messages confuse
        please tell me one thing straight

        what will take me further

3.03    krishna:

        as i said ages ago
        two paths:
            knowledge (samkhya)
            action (karma yoga)

3.04

            but
        doing nothing doesn't mean
        you're free from karma

        nor does renunciation
        mean you're anywhere
        near enlightenment

3.05

            'coz   in fact
        not for a moment
        do you do
        nothing

        doing's what you're made to do
        not in your control

        by nature
        inborn

3.06     s/he who represses     senses  organs
         while mind fondles     pleasures
                  hypocrite!
         fools herself

3.07     (but) s/he who's detached &
         harnesses senses  actions  organs
         with the mind

         is better

3.08     do what you have to do
         rather than not

         if nothing's done
         even the body won't run

3.09     in this world
         all activity except *yagna*     (sacred fire rite
                                          oblation to the divine  but
                                          you'll soon see it's a metaphor
                                          for a way of living)

         creates a chain    cycle of karma

         so that's how you've got to do it
         ritual   detached   free

3.10     way back after
         creating humans
         via yagna

         said prajapati     (a creator mentioned in the vedas)
         by yagna may you flourish
         let yagna be your wishing cow

3.11

by yagna
may you nourish the deities
may the deities nourish you

being   together   for each other
you'll get there   all's well

3.12

pleased by the yagna the
deities will give you
what you like

(caution:) s/he who enjoys her gifts
without reciprocating
is a thief

3.13

those who are true
eat leftovers       (after offering the yagna)
they're freed from problems

the wretched       cook for their own sake
feed on misery

3.14

living beings
↓ from
food
↓
rain
↓
yagna
↓
action / duties

(life's based on action)

3.15        the first rites  action  arose
            from brahman

            brahman
            arose as *om*        (the undying creation sound)
            & spread  so

            the omnipresent is ever
            rooted in yagna

3.16        thus   arjuna   the wheel
            was set in motion

                                those who don't move it along
                                        hedonists
                                        troublemakers
                                live in vain      but

3.17        s/he whose joy is
            her divine self (the embodied timeless "it" we discussed before)
                        satisfied
                        content
            doesn't feel the pressure

3.18        the question
                        to do or not to do
            doesn't come up

            s/he doesn't have an agenda
            or need anyone

3.19        so  do what has to be done
            always detached   that's
            how you'll get
            to the ultimate goal

3.20          king janaka   (for instance)
              made it   to perfection
              through work

              if only for the sake of
              the world      to keep it running
              you're to work

                        (me too  for example)

3.21          a leader sets the standard

              whatever s/he does
              everyone follows

3.22          there's nothing for me
              to do in the three worlds
              no unfinished business
              to be done

              yet i keep at it   i work

3.23          if i did not carry on
              tireless

              neither would anyone

3.24          if i did not do my bit
              these worlds would collapse
                        i would be the cause of
              chaos
              these people  destroyed

3.25          the ignorant cling
              to what they do

              the wise must work   detached
              for the sake of the world collective

3.26          don't mess with the minds
of ignoramuses
entangled in their work

in fact  help them  let them
enjoy all that they do
& you stay on course

3.27          nature is the work of
the properties of matter     nature is  the nature of nature

the egoist  (literally "i am the doer")
takes the credit

3.28               arjuna
s/he who knows
how it works
nature & events  roleplay
how properties inhere in matter    natura naturans
is not attached

3.29          those fooled by the ways of nature
are attached to its actions
let them be

those who know it all
must not disturb the dull
who don't know the whole story

3.30               just leave it all up to me
mind inward
desireless
undifferent to possession
unfrenzied
fight!

3.31      those who practice this  my teaching
                    in earnest
                    without cynicism
          are free from karma

3.32               but note
          those who don't
                    cynical
                    confused by any knowledge
                    thoughtless
          are ruined

3.33      so each            even the wise
          acts according to nature

          living beings
          follow their nature

          what good will repression do

3.34               a sense organ's
          attraction
          aversion
                    hooked
                    to its object

          don't be seduced by them
          they're obstacles
          in your way

3.35      take responsibility
          do your duty   even if it isn't nice
          rather than another's role well done

          better to die
          in your own work
          than to risk danger
          in another's

3.36    arjuna:

> then why does one go wrong   krishna
> although unwilling
> & even as if coerced

3.37    krishna:

> this "anger"
> this "desire"
>> comes from *rajas*
>>> (pleasure loving nature explained in detail later)
> note   voracious & heinous
> this   here   is enemy

3.38

> as fire enveloped by smoke
> mirror by dust
> embryo by womb
>
> this
>  is masked by
> that

3.39

> knowledge   even in the wise
> is obscured
> by desire ... lust
>
> fire insatiable
> ever enemy

3.40

> & its address?
> the senses  mind  intellect!
>
> it's by using them that it
> blocks your knowledge
> confuses  seduces  you
>> who are in a body  and encased in them

3.41          restraining your senses  et al
              determined as a bull  arjuna

              destroy desire              the wretch
                                          it destroys
                                          knowledge  wisdom

3.42          they call sense organs great  but

              mind is greater than senses
              intellect is greater than mind

              & you
              even greater than intellect

3.43                                      so
              knowing who
              tops the intellect

              support your self
              by yourself

              as for this enemy        in the guise of desire
                                       hard to face
              arjuna
                 destroy it!

4.01          about this method        everlasting yoga
              i told vivasvat (sun) who
              told manu (first human) who
              told ikshvaku (his son)

4.02          passed on this way       that's how
              the best of seers knew of it

              by time   on earth
              vast
              was lost  arjuna

4.03         this ancient yoga
        is top secret

        i only told you
        as my devotee
        & friend

4.04     arjuna:         but
        your birth was later
        vivasvat's earlier

        how can i believe
        you said it first

4.05     krishna:
        many  my past lives
        yours too

        i know them
        you don't

4.06                   although
        i am     birthless deathless
        god of all

        by my creativity
        i direct my own nature  &
        lo      here i wholly am

4.07     arjuna

        when the correct fades
              incorrect rises

        i procreate myself

4.08
full on
i am
from time to time    to
                    save good people
                    crackdown on evil
                    settle what's right

4.09
s/he who realizes
my divinity          in birth & action
                    when s/he leaves body
comes to me
                    not to rebirth

4.10
mind full of me
depending fully on me

by the practice of wisdom
purified

passionangerfearless

many have become
one with me

4.11
who        what        they ask
them        that        i serve
                        you get what you ask for
all ways are mine
                        regardless of what path
                        you follow
                        me

4.12    wanting success
        in what they do

        people
        make offerings
        to deities

        worldly success comes quick
        from these activities

4.13    the four "castes"  sorted by traits & tasks
        were issued by me
                    yet note
        i am      a constant        my energy infinite  everlasting
        a non doer

4.14    what i do does not stain me
        for i have no desire
        for the fruit of action

                    s/he who knows just this of me
                    is as free

4.15    bygone seekers
        knew this &
        followed my example

        so should you

4.16    what is/isn't action
        even poets
        are perplexed

        i'll explain

        knowing better
        you'll be free from dullness

4.17
you've got to know
what is action  what is
incorrect action  what is
non action
        the ways of action are
        hard to fathom

4.18
s/he who spots
non action in
what looks like action

action in
what looks like not

is by far smarter
connected        yogi
in everything s/he does

4.19
s/he whose
projects are without
greedy motives

work primed
in knowledge-fire

the wise call pundit

4.20
s/he who

giving up the clinging
to profit

content
undependent

even when busy  in fact
accrues no karma

4.21        s/he who
wishlessly
           mind  self  under control
           giving up acquisition
works only with body
is not culpable

4.22        content   whatever the gain

not swinging to opposites   pleasure pain

envyfree

in success unsuccess
equanimous

although working
is unbound      no karma

4.23        s/he whose
           work is free from expectations
           mind anchored in knowledge
work = yagna
karma dissolves

4.24        s/he whose actions are absorbed in brahman

        food = brahman/offering/god
        eating = brahman/process/god
        digesting fire = brahman/fire /god
        eater = brahman/god

goes to brahman

4.25         some yogis do the ritual yagna
to a deity

others offer
to this fire of brahman

4.26         some offer sense pleasures   hearing etcetera
to discipline-fires

        (burn pleasures in discipline
        = give them up)

others offer sense objects   sound etcetera
to sense-fires

        (senses consume objects
        so senses are like fires)

4.27         some offer all actions of the senses
& of the *prana*     (*qi*  energy  breath of life regulated by breath)
into the fire of self discipline
kindled by wisdom

        (however you live
        your life is yagna
        if you make it so)

4.28         yagnas galore:
        material things
        austerities
        yogic practices
& for ascetics with strict vows
        self study
        knowledge

4.29
    controlling breath   keen to
    control prana
    some cycle
    inhalation into exhalation
    exhalation into inhalation
        (yogic breathing practices)

4.30
    those who restrict diet
    burn breath in prana     (body ... to spirit)

    all these ways work
    & their errors are destroyed by yagna

4.31
    those who consecrate food to deities
        what's left
        is manna
    go to brahman

    those who offer nothing
    don't even get by in this world
        where's the question
        of another world

4.32
    different yagnas are thus
    laid at the mouth of brahman

    they all come from activity

    note that
    & you will be liberated

4.33
    dedicating knowledge    to brahman
    is better than giving up material things

    all actions   none excluded
    are included in knowledge

4.34              knowers  seers  of truth
                        will give you  knowledge        so
                                             submit humbly
                                           interrogate
                                           serve

4.35              you won't get
                        confused again

                        you'll see   without exception
                        all beings in yourself
                        & then in me

4.36              even if you are
                        the worst of evildoers

                        you'll cross evil
                        with knowledge-plank

4.37              fire ignited turns wood to ash
                        knowledge-fire turns karma to ash

4.38              there's nothing in this world as
                        pure as knowledge

                        one who is perfected in yoga     in time
                        knows knowledge in oneself

4.39              the faithful one gets knowledge
                                    holding it as highest
                                      & restraining sense organs
                      & goes to super peace
                      without delay

4.40       the ignorant
the faithless
the doubter      is lost
      neither this world nor
      the beyond nor
      happiness

(to sum up)

4.41       s/he who      actions renounced in yoga
      doubt severed by knowledge
      self possessed
          actions don't bind

therefore

4.42       sever the doubt in your heart   originating in ignorance
with knowledge sword  &  having cut away this doubt
      go yoga!
      stand up! arjuna

5.01    arjuna:
      krishna  first you say
      renunciation of activity  then
      you say activity

      what's better  which one
      tell me for sure

5.02    krishna:
      both are best     causes of the
      nothing's-better-than-this
      state
      especially
      the path of activity

35

5.03            s/he who
                     beyond opposites
           neither desires nor hates

           is ever-the-yogi
           freed easy from
           ties     responsibilities

5.04            the inexperienced   not wise
           call these
           two paths two
           different directions  but

           either followed well
           finds the same results

5.05            karma yoga goes
           where samkhya
           does

           the two are one

           s/he who can see that
           has insight

5.06            renunciation is hard to get to
           without first training in
           karma yoga
                    but  arjuna
           the yogi who's fastened
           to karma yoga
           gets there fast   to brahman

5.07            dedicated to
           purified by  karma yoga

           in command       of oneself
                            of sense organs

seeing one self
in everyone

although working
is untainted        no karma

5.08       i do nothing   thinks
           the attuned yogi   when
           seeinghearingtouchingsmellingeatingwalkingsleepingbreathing

5.09       talkingexcretingcatching&openingclosingeyes

           certain that senses  organs
           only exist in their objects

5.10       s/he who offers
           all activities to brahman
           giving up attachment  is

           unmarked by negativity
           like a lotusleaf by water

5.11–12    the yogi works  with body mind intellect
           or only with senses
           forsaking
           attachment & results
           for self purification

           reaches peace

                   due to selfish desires
                   the non yogi is bound
                   to be attached
                   to consequences

5.13      forsaking ownership of all actions
with the mind

in command of oneself

sits relaxed in her place (body)
of nine gates     (ears 2 eyes 2 nostrils 2
mouth 1 anus 1 genital gate 1
= 9)

5.14      neither does
nor causes to be done

(but let's be clear)
i'm no agent (either)     for actions
& consequences

come together
by nature

5.15      i do not receive
"bad" & "good"
knowledge is hidden
by lack of knowledge
that's why people get confused

5.16      knowledge     sun
removes lack of    illuminates
knowledge      ultimate
reality

5.17      mind set on this
as both foundation & goal

faults dusted off by knowledge

no return to rebirth

5.18      pundits see unity in all:
                    a humble scholar priest
                    a cow an elephant
                    a dog & a dog-
                    cooking outcaste

5.19      s/he whose mind
                    is fixed in unity
          is with brahman
                    perfect unity
          & conquers rebirth
          right here

5.20      don't rejoice      when you get what you like
          don't shudder      when you don't

                    firm in thought
                    unshakeable
          the brahman-knower's
                    rooted
          in brahman

5.21      s/he who knows happiness
          within herself
          undependent
          on external things

          attached to brahman
          via yoga   s/he
          reaches joy  everlasting

5.22      pleasures born of contact
                    are wombs of pain          o arjuna  son of kunti
          begin
          & end

          the wise person doesn't
          enjoy them

5.23           only s/he
who can endure
the stirrings of lust & anger        right here when
in the body

is an attuned
a happy person

5.24           in joy with in overjoy with in light with in brahman
the yogi reaches brahmanirvana

5.25           errorless
doubtfree
oneself under control
        sages who rejoice
        in the welfare of all beings
attain brahmanirvana

5.26           the lustfree angerfree
self controlled thought controlled
self knower's
brahmanirvana
        is at hand

5.27           ousting worldly contact

gaze in   between eyebrows

inbreath & outbreath
regulated in the nostrils    (yogic breathing *pranayama*)

5.28           the seeker         with the highest goal   liberation
                       without desire fear anger
                       mind thought senses reined in
is everfree

5.29           knowing me       vast god of all worlds
                                   a friend   in the heart   of all beings
                                   eater  receiver
                                   of offerings in yagnas & penances

           reaches peace

6.01     krishna:

           s/he who
           does     duties  rituals
                   without banking on the results
                   is a *sanyasi* a yogi

           doesn't
                isn't

6.02           "renunciation"
           is yoga

           no one's a yogi
           without renouncing
           self interest

6.03           for the seeker
           who wants to advance   be yogi
           karmayoga   selfless activity
           is the way

           for the advanced yogi
           equanimity is the way

6.04           when s/he isn't attached    to actions
                                        sense objects
           has renounced self interest

           s/he's said to have
           stepped up to
           yoga

41

6.05–6.06      you've got to
help yourself up      not      put yourself down
you are your own            you are your own
friend                             enemy

s/he who has self mastery  s/he who hasn't
is her own friend                 is her own enemy

6.07      for the selfmastered peaceful you
the divine            (literally, the ultimate you)
is immediate  accessible
            in cold heat
            happiness unhappiness
            honor dishonor

6.08–6.09            s/he who is content
in knowledge   understanding
who's on top of things   controlling senses
attuned to her inner self

yoked =
= yogi

for her                          dirt = stone = gold
it's all the same
s/he's the same   to      friend ~ foe
                                relative ~ enemy
                                good ~ bad

6.10      a yogi must always be yoked to  focused on
her inner self

keep to herself

alone
self controlled    (even) in thought

wanting nothing  ↔  having nothing

6.11        founding  a clean place a steady seat  not too high
                                           not too low

                (layers:)
                  <u>cloth</u>
             <u>antelope skin</u>
            <u>kusa holy grass</u>

6.12        sitting there       mind focused
                        thought & senses arrested
        practice yoga for self purification

6.13                | neck
                | head
                | back
                in line
                steady no motion
        gazing at your
        nosetip   nowhere else

6.14        quiet  fearless
        firmly celibate

        yoked  controlling mind
        thinking of me   as ideal

        sit

6.15        ever disciplined
        mind controlled

        the yogi arrives
        at peace  nirvana

        is one with me

6.16    yoga's not possible
        for one who      overeats
                         fasts
                         oversleeps or
                         stays up all night

6.17    balanced  yoked in       food 'n entertainment
                                 activities
                                 sleeping waking
        yoga kills depression

6.18     when s/he's

        mind controlled
        innerself absorbed
        desireless to all desires

        s/he's said to be yoked  disciplined

6.19    there's a simili
        for a mindcontrolled yogi
        focused on yoga:

        a lamp unflickering
        a windless place

6.20    when the mind stops roaming
        checked by yoga

        & when you see yourself  thus
                 ohhappy!

6.21    that infinite joy
        that's understood by intelligence
        that's beyond the senses

s/he knows
& on that basis
proceeds

6.22  having got there s/he knows
  nothing's better to get

  rooted in that s/he's
  unruffled
  by big troubles

6.23  yoga  lets you off
    the pain hook

  so persevere practice
  think positive

6.24  use your mind

  drop desires all no exception
  that come
  from your will

  restrain all your senses totally

6.25  s l o w l y cease
  activity

  use intellect to
  hold on to steadiness

  fix mind on you who you really are

  mustn't think
  of any thing else

6.26
where   wanders
the restless  fickle
mind

there      rein in
bring back  under control
to you

6.27
the calm yogi
has the best bliss
even her passion's calm
faultless
become brahman

6.28
thus always in yoga
the yogi  blemish free
taps into brahman  easy  just like that
no end to joy!

6.29
sees her self in all beings
all beings in her self

self same everywhere

6.30
s/he who sees me everywhere      for her i am never gone
& everything in me              s/he is never gone for me

6.31
anchored in unity              however s/he is  s/he is
s/he serves me in all beings              in me

6.32
s/he who          whether up or down
by relating everything to herself
sees unity everywhere:

"super yogi"

6.33     arjuna:

this yoga you talk of
equanimity
steady staying

restless i   don't see it

6.34

mind's restless
stubborn strong   extreme
staying it   i believe
as trying as trying
to stay wind

6.35     krishna:              o strong armed arjuna

no doubt the mind's moves are hard to stay
you get a grip      by practice &
undifference

6.36

hard to get   if you're self uncontrolled

not   if you're self controlled
if you systematically
try

6.37     arjuna:

s/he who has faith
but no discipline

mind strayed from yoga
success in yoga unfound

where does s/he go   krishna

6.38

a dropout in both worlds
anchorless
confused on the way
of brahman

does s/he vanish   like a torn cloud

6.39
only you can clear my doubt   krishna
totally
there's none
other than you

6.40    krishna:

arjuna
s/he who does good things
isn't lost          in this world or that
doesn't end up badly

6.41
the interrupted yogi

gets to the worlds of do-gooders
lives there for ages is
born again   in a
home of the holyfamous

6.42
or in a family
of wise yogis

this kind of birth
not easy to get
in this world

6.43
& there   reconnects
to wisdom
of previous life

from there s/he
tries again
for success          o arjuna son of the kuru clan

6.44      s/he's driven
by previous practice
as if without will

is curious
about yoga

& goes beyond
just vedic recitations

6.45      by trying by controlling
the mind
the yogi's cleansed of faults

perfected across births
then goes
to the goal

6.46      a yogi's better than     an ascetic
      scholar
      ritualist
     yogi be! arjuna

6.47      &   of all yogis  s/he

whose very core   whose heart
goes out to me

who  devoted    serves me
is most connected to me

7.01      hear how
      me on your mind
      practicing yoga
      trusting me    without doubt
you'll totally know me

7.02        to you i'll give
knowledge + understanding

of that which
when you know

nothing
will remain
to be known

7.03        not even one in a thousand people
tries to be perfect

of those who try
& those who achieve

barely anyone
knows me truly

7.04        eight parts to
my manifest nature

earth water fire wind
ether        (energy field)
mind intellect
ego

7.05        & that's not a big deal

my other nature
the ultimate  it
supports the forms of life   is the
                   womb of beings

*Mani Rao*

7.06–7.11                              everyone! get that

# I AM

the origin
the end  of
the entire universe


there's no thing higher

it's all strung on me
pearls on a string

water's flavor       light in moon  sun   om in all vedas

sound in etheric space

spunk in humans
the nice fragrance on earth
sun's brilliance
life in all living
penance in ascetics

know me                      ancient   timeless seed
intelligence of the intelligent
radiance of the radiant

strength of the strong
who are desire & passion free
the love in beings
that isn't inappropriate

51

7.12            (& the three qualities *gunas*)
                 sattva    (~ clarity
                 rajas     ~ passion
                 tamas     ~ inertia)
they're from me

i'm not in them
they're in me

7.13            the whole world is
made of these three

so it's fooled
under their influence

doesn't quite know i am
beyond these

constant

7.14            this  my
divine play      made of gunas

my mystery     magic     maya
hard to fathom

only those who
hang on to me
get past maya

7.15        fools   wrongdoers
            the meanest
            don't seek me

            wisdom warped
            by maya

            their lifestyle
            demonic

7.16        four kinds of rightdoers
            worship me
                    the suffering
                    seekers of knowledge / success
                    & the wise

7.17                    among them the wise
                        always attuned            i love her  &
                        noted for singular devotion   s/he loves me

7.18        they're all fine but
                        the wise one is  thought of as
                        my quintessence

                        united s/he
                        sticks with me   the ultimate goal

7.19                    at the end of many lives
                        the wise one    one so good   is hard to find
                        turns to me:
                        "krishna's everything"

7.20        people go to other deities
            with this & that wish
            this & that ritual
            they're limited
            by their own nature

7.21    it is i who grant
        unshakeable faith  to

        whoever prefers   to revere
        whatever deity

7.22    it is i who give her
        what s/he wants

        when s/he worships (her fave)
        with this faith

7.23    but limited are the gains
        for little brains

        those who worship deities
        go to deities

        my devotees come to me   only

7.24    the unintelligent believe i     formless
        am obvious

        without knowing my ultimate state
                constant
                supreme

7.25    i am     not visible to everyone
                masked by my mystic powers

        the world    duh
        doesn't realize
        i am       birthless
                constant   undying

7.26    i know those  who have gone
            who are now
            & will be
    no one knows me

7.27    due to
    duality  delusion
        desire   aversion

    all
    fall   into
    when they are born

7.28    but those with good deeds
          errors at an end
    freed from dualities

    adore me with firm vows

7.29    those who count on me
    for liberation  from old age & death

    they know it all    brahman
             action &
             the highest self

7.30    they who know
    i am
        the divine    fundamental being
        the manifest
        the fundamental yagna

    even when it's time
    to leave  (to "die")
        (they're not in panic)
    they have presence of mind
    (for) they know me

8.01    arjuna:

        huh    what exactly is this brahman      o supreme
        ultimate me
                karma   action
                   manifest
                        divine fundamental

8.02

                            fundamental sacrifice
                where in this body  how
      & how at the time of death
      can you be known
           by these oh so selfcontrolled types

8.03    krishna:

      "brahman" is undying ultimate

      "the ultimate self" is who you really are

      creation is action / procreation karma

      gives rise to existence beingness

8.04      manifest  is what dies

      divine fundamental is  the ultimate being    me

      i am the fundamental yagna in the body    your body arjuna

8.05      s/he who
      at the end
      when going
      out of body
      contemplates me
      goes to my state
      of being  no doubt

8.06
&
what s/he contemplates
is what s/he attains

8.07
so
think of me always   & fight
offering your mind & thought
to me you'll reach me   no doubt

8.08
mind focused by yoga practice
undistracted

contemplates the ultimate being
& makes it there

8.09
s/he who recalls   the firstpoet
governor
who anchors all
subtler than atom
of unimaginable form
suncomplexion   beyond darkness

8.10
when it's time   mind steady
to move on   charged with devotion & yogapower
life energy entering nicely
between the brows
goes to the ultimate being

8.11
i'll give you a quick brief about this path
that the vedasavvy call undying
that passionfree ascetics embark on
that those who want follow in celibacy

8.12–13    s/he who
                        all bodygates under control    (nine, remember)
                        mind arrested in the heart's intense feeling

                        life energy at the top of the head
                        in steady focused yoga
                        utters the one-syllabic om
            contemplates me

            giving up the body goes
            to the ultimate place

8.14       for the ever-yoked  yogi
                        ever remembering me
                        mind never elsewhere
            i'm easy

8.15       great perfected beings
                        who come to me
            don't go to that sad transient place: rebirth

8. 16      there's rebirth in all the created worlds
            under *brahma*  (the creator
                        one of the team of three
                        creator preserver destroyer
                        & different from the over & above
                        brahman)
            but once you reach me   there's none

8.17       brahma's day = 1,000 ages
            brahma's night = 1,000 ages
                        (an age = over 4 million earth years)

            those who know that
            know what day & night really mean

8.18      all the manifest came from an unmanifest
at the start of this day

at the start of this night they'll
dissolve   "unmanifest" again

8.19      these hordes of beings   having been again&again
dissolve   can't help it
when it's night

& re-be
when it's day

8.20      but there's another unmanifest
beyond this unmanifest

when all beings
dissolve   it doesn't

8.21      called the undying
the ultimate destination

once there
you're not coming back   it's my
home

8.22      this is the ultimate divine being
         anchors all beings &
         permeates the universe
reached
by devotion      no other way

8.23      i'll tell about a
departure time that tells
if a yogi will be
reborn or not

8.24–8.26
when the sun's       when the sun's
in the north        in the south
when it's bright day light  when it's smoke dark night
when the moon's waxing  when the moon's waning

those who know brahman  the yogi goes to moon light
go to brahman        &is reborn
no rebirth

the path of light     the path of darkness

these are considered given

8.27
the yogi knows
isn't confused

always be steady arjuna
in yoga

8.28
knowing all this
the yogi goes beyond

the (limited) uses of
vedas yagnas penances
charity

goes to the ultimate
the original place

9.01–9.02
you're uncynical so
i'll tell you

a knowledge + understanding a

top secret  hi science  pure  best
evident  easy  irreducible

a law (spiritual)
to release you from error

9.03            those who have no faith in this
don't make it to me

they're reborn
to death   the way of the world

9.04–05        my unmanifest
permeates the universe

all beings are anchored on me      not i on them
                        & yet not in me   i am
                                    their cause  sustenance
                                    independent
                    see my awesome power!

9.06            as wind  vast      blows everywhere but
                            always fixed
to the sky

on me
all beings rely

              imagine!

9.07–9.08      at the end of the day      a brahma day
all beings go back into my matter

at the beginning of a new day
i turn to nature  my material

& come up        again & again
with these hordes of beings   automatic
                              shaped by
                              nature

9.09            nor do these activities
tie me down

coolly detached  i sit

9.10
    i keep an eye over
matternature    who conceives
        animate inanimate
it's how the universe turns

9.11–12
    fools give no cred
↓        to my human form
thoughtless    not knowing my
hopeless    true state
activities pointless    mighty god
knowledge useless    of all beings

demonic
    it's their nature to be fooled

9.13–14
    great beings
live in divine nature

undistracted    they know me  the everlasting one
they serve me    as the origin of beings
always
sing my praises
greet me
adore me  with devotion

always reined in
with firm vows  they keep trying

9.15
    & others
by the yagna of knowledge

worship me    who knows all
as one
as many

9.16–19     I the yagna fire chant ritual offertory butter
           herb oblation
father of the universe mother founder grandpa pure om three
           vedas to be known

destination carrier witness resthouse divinity refuge friend
           origin end
maintenance treasury seed everlasting

i heat rain refrain exude am death immortality i am
           and i am  not

9.20–21     those who
know three vedas
drink nectar
adore me &
errors purified
by yagna they seek
heaven destination

to the world of the gods they go    heaven
enjoy joys divine

then
running out of credit they
return to the world of mortals

it's the law of the vedas
followed

back & forth
wanting & getting

63

9.22    but for those who think of me    no other
who worship me
& for the disciplined among them

i personally
bring them what they don't have
preserve what they do

9.23    even those who adore other deities
with dedication devotion
             although on a tangent
really adore me

9.24    it is i who relish    eat at  all
yagnas

they don't recognize me    truly
so they fail    they

9.25    who honor deities go to deities
who honor ancestors to ancestors
spirits to spirits
me to me

9.26    s/he who offers
steady devotion
             a flower
             a fruit
             some water
             a leaf (a page!)
pure love
             i eat

9.27    whatever you do    give    eat    offer
whatever your austerities

offer it to me

9.28        be disciplined
            renounce

            you'll be freed
                    from good & bad   fruits of actions
            & come to me

9.29                    i'm the same to all
                       no favorites /hatreds
                       but (it's just that)

            those who worship
            me with devotion
                    they are in me
                    i am in them

9.30–32     oh even the bad       if s/he worships me & no other
                                  is considered  good  well done  for s/he
            soon becomes good
            & peaceful

                    know this!
            not a single one
            of my devotees
            is lost

9.33–34    all    women
              vaisyas (third "caste")
              sudras (fourth "caste")
              people born to lawless mothers
           who rely on me
           reach the ultimate destination

              compare how easy then
              for a pure *brahmin* (first "caste"  not brahman)
              or devoted sage

           it's a sad transient world
           put your mind on me adore me worship me

           tuned up you'll
           come to me
                          your goal

10.01     my dear arjuna
          i want your welfare  so

          again  listen  i'll say
          the last word on this

10.02     even sages & deities
          have no clue       don't know my
          i am their         origin

10.03     originless
          birthless
          i
          mighty deity  of the world

              s/he who knows this is
              among mortals is
              unconfused
              freed
              from all errors

10.04–05  intelligence / wisdom / clarity / endurance / self restraint /
          happiness / sadness / equanimity / contentment / truth /
          peace / nonviolence / austerity / charity / fear /
          fearlessness/ fame / notoriety / be ing / unbe ing /
          in all beings
          these states of being
          are my many ways

10.06     the seven sages from way back
          the four manus    from whom these beings of this
          world came to be came from my mind

10.07     s/he who knows this
          truth     my manifestation   achievement
          is attuned
          via steady yoga    no doubt

10.08     full of feeling     i am the origin of
          the intelligent     everything
          worship me so     revolves from me

10.09     with me on their mind
          life energy focused on me
          enjoying   being content

          chatting about me
          enlightening each other   about me

10.10     & those who     among them
                    always disciplined
          worship me   with love

          i give them the intelligence
                    they use
          to come to me

10.11

        i      empathizing with them
              from within them
remove the darkness      that comes from ignorance
with the lamp of knowledge

10.12–18
   arjuna:

uber brahman final destination utter purity eternal
divine person original deity birthless omnipresent

     that's what they say   all the sages divine sage narada & asita
devala vyasa  & you say so yourself

               i believe
                 it is
              all true

     what you say krishna for sure neither the deities nor the demons
know your manifestation
               you're your own evidence

     best man  source of everyone's welfare deity of all beings  deity
of deities  master of the universe

     you've got to reveal your divine your manifestations how do you
do it permeating the worlds and yet located in it

     how can i know you o yogi o krishna by thinking of you
constantly (i suppose but) in what states how o god how am i to
imagine you

     tell me more about yourself your power & manifestation speak
again your words are nectar       i haven't had enough

10.19            krishna:

on with it then   i'll tell you
my divine manifestations
but only the main ones  for arjuna
there's no end to my spread


10.20                    I AM the YOU
in the heart of all beings
i am the beginning i am the middle & the end i am


10.21-32                    vishnu among adityas
sun among lights
marichi among maruts
moon among the constellations of the night
sama veda among vedas
vasava among deities
mind among senses
awareness among beings
siva among rudras
kubera among yaksas & raksasas
pavaka among the vasus
meru among mountains
head priest
priest of the deities
skanda among army chiefs
ocean among water bodies
brighu among sages  om among sounds
chant among yagnas
among the unmovable the himalayas
holy fig among the trees
narada among divine sages
citraratha among gandharvas
kapila among achiever yogis
born from nectar (in oceanchurn)
ucchaishravas among horses
airavat among king elephants
king among people
thunderbolt among weapons

wishing cow among cows
kandarpa the begetter
vasuki among serpents
ananta among the naga snakes
varuna among water beings
aryaman  among ancestors
death among controllers
prahalada among daityas
time among calculators
king of beasts among beasts
vainateya among birds
wind among purifiers
rama among weaponweilders
makara among sea ferocities
ganga among rivers


i am
the beginning the middle & the end
of creations


the logic among debators
knowledge among knowledges: self knowledge

10.33–34                       "A" among alphabets
combination in compound words


only i
am infinite time
creator omniscient
i am death  all-destructive
source of what will be
among femininities:
fame speech beauty
wisdom endurance memory
& constancy

10.35–38
brhatsama among sama chants
gayatri among meters
(cool) november among months
flowery spring among seasons
gambling of the dishonest
radiance of the radiant
victory
effort
good's goodness
vasudeva among vrsnis

& i am you   arjuna  among pandavas

among sages vyasa
among poets  usanas
clout of rulers
advice for those who want to win
silence among secrets
knowledge of the knowledgeable

10.39
i am the seed of all beings
animate inanimate
without me nothing could be

10.40
there's no end
to my manifestations
divinity

all these examples
extent
of my manifestations

10.41
in every instance
whatever's powerful glorious lively
is a part of my glory

10.42          but what's the point of
               so much knowledge   arjuna

               i support the universe
               with so little of my self

11.01    arjuna:
               my confusion's gone
               you've kindly
               told me the secret
               spirit-ual

11.02          i heard in detail from you    krishna
                         irreducible awesomeness
               how beings come to be
               and un-be

11.03          so this   what you describe   krishna
               i'd like to see

               your divine form

11.04          if you believe i can          (withstand it)
               krishna   please
               show me
               your infinite

11.05    krishna:
               see my divine forms   arjuna
               hundreds   or rather thousands

               all sorts of
               colors & shapes

11.06          see        the (celestials) vasus adityas maruts rudras & asvins
               how many
               wow never seen before

11.07          here  arjuna
               see now  with me

               the entire universe
               in my body

               animate inanimate
               & whatever else you want to see

11.08          oh you're unable
               to see me with your eyes

               ok  i give you
               a divine eye
               now see
               my divine power

11.09  sanjaya (to dhrtarashta) :
       & then vishnu the powerful (krishna) showed his ultimate divine form
       to arjuna

11.10          myriad mouths  eyes
                       divine jewelries
                       raised weaponries
                               what a sight

11.11          in divine garlands & clothes
                       perfumes & balms
               infinite
                       omniscient          facing all directions
                               at once  ah   all wondrous

11.12          if a thousand suns rise
               together in the sky
                       imagine that
                               that   the brilliance of this awesome one

11.13
    there  with krishna
    arjuna saw
        in the body
        of the god of gods
    a diverse one universe

11.14
    arjuna
        overcome by surprise
            goose bumps
    bowing his head
    said   reverentially

11.15
    omigod  i see        in your body    deities
                    a gathering of all sorts of beings
                    brahma seated on a lotus
                    divine serpents & all the sages

11.16
    i see    you everywhere  infinite form
        myriad eyes arms bellies faces

        no end no middle no beginning

    i see    the deity of the universe
        the universe   its form

11.17
    i see    you    so hard to see
                in totality

            with a crown club discus

        blazes
            sun      fire      radiance

            infinite

        mass of light

            shining everywhere

11.18     i get it    you're    the highest goal of knowledge
   the deepest anchor of the world

   everlasting   undying
   defender of eternal law

   the original one

11.19     i see     you     without beginning middle end

   infinite arms
        infinite strength

   your eyes  the sun & moon
       your mouth  a blazing pyre

   by your brilliance   the universe afire

11.20     in all directions  you o
   solo you fill the whole
   between heaven & earth

   the three worlds   (earth heaven & inbetween)
   shudder
   at this     a terrible marvel
   form

11.21     there     hordes of deities
       (i see)    going into you  they're
   terrified they
   praise you
   make reverent signs

   hordes of great
   accomplished sages
   they say hello  they
   praise you profusely  in hymns

11.22   they  the adityas the rudras vasus & sadhyas
       see  all the deities of the universe
       you  the asvins the maruts the ancestors
           hordes of gandharvas yakshas demons
           & the accomplished

           & they're all bewildered

11.23   seeing your myriad
              mouths eyes arms thighs feet
              bellies & gory teeth
           the worlds shudder &
           so do i

11.24   seeing you a blaze a spectrum
           touching the sky

           mouth agape fiery
           expansive eyes o vishnu

           i tremble within i find no
           peace i can't stand it

11.25   seeing your mouths your gory tusks like
              the end of time blaze

           i don't know where i am
           i can't find a place
              have mercy!
           deity of deities
           home of the universe

11.26   there  all of dhrtarashtra's sons with
       (i see) hordes of kings
           bhisma drona karna
             & our main warriors too

11.27                    they rush  into your mouths
                             tusks  gory  scary
                    some caught between your teeth
                          ugh! see  crushed heads

11.28                    the heroes of the human world
                    enter your blazing mouths
                                as river currents
                             run  to the ocean

11.29                the worlds hurry into your mouths
                to be destroyed
                          frenzied moths
                        to flame

11.30                    all around you devour you lick
                    all the worlds
                    with your fiery mouths

                    (while) your brilliance fills
                        the worlds
                    your rays consume them

11.31   tell me who you are  sir
                    o so ferocious
                    *saluts* to you
                    o best of deities
                          mercy

             i want to know  original one
                 about your ways
             i have no clue

11.32 krishna:

        i am time   the force
        that does the world in

        i've come to annihilate
        the worlds

        even without you (killing them)
        they     positioned on the opposite side
        will not be

11.33        so stand up  get some cred
        conquer enemies  then enjoy the office

            they've been killed by me already
        you just be   arjuna
        an instrument

11.34        drona bhishma jayadrata karna & other war heroes
             have been killed by me  so
           kill     don't flounder
           fight    you'll conquer the enemies
               in the war

11.35   sanjaya (to dhrtarashta) : hearing krishna's words  a shaken
arjuna   reverential
handsfolding  fearful  bowed  stammered again

11.36   arjuna:
        it's appropriate
            that the universe celebrate
            & enjoy your fame
            that demons  scared run here & there

11.37
           & why shouldn't they
           you're the
      original creator   greater
      than brahma

deity of deities
infinite
home of the universe   you're
undying
       what is   what isn't   & beyond

11.38
you're
first deity   the ancient one
this universe's deepest anchor

the knower
the to-be-known   the final destination

your infinite form    permeates
the universe

11.39
you are   the deities
wind death fire water moon

prajapati

first ancestor

salaam to you      a thousand times
      & again  salaam   salaam

11.40
salaam  from the front   from the back
from all sides surround  salaam  (o omniscient)
      (to) endless boundless valor & force
you are the end of everything
     so you are everything

11.41        from ignorance  of your power
                tipsiness
                        or fondness
      i've been rash
      said whatnot      "hey krishna  hey yaduboy  hey buddy"

      thought you (just) friend

11.42        if for jokes' sake   when we went out
      i've treated you         or lay back
      disrespectfully               or sat around or ate
             in privacy or  good lord  in front of others

      i beg pardon   o unfathomable

11.43        you're the father of the world      of the animate inanimate
          its worshipped
          weighty teacher
      there's nothing like you  in the three worlds
          so how could there be anything better than you
      o of incomparable glory

11.44        so i salute i prostrate
               be generous o laudable god
         bear with me as  father to son
                   friend to friend
                     lover to beloved

11.45–46                          i'm happy enough  seeing the previously unseen
                                           (but) my mind's in panic  shaken
                       have mercy o god of gods o home of the universe
                       o god  show me that form

                                           with a crown
                                           a club
                                           discus in hand

                                                i want to see you only like that
                              o universe of forms
                              o thousand armed    become
                              four armed

11.47      god :

                              pleased with you
                              this ultimate form        an endless brilliant original universe
                              was displayed
                                      by my power

                              that hasn't been seen by anyone else before

11.48                    i can't be seen in this form
                         by anyone other than by you   arjuna  o hero of the kurus
                         in the human world
                                   whether via veda yagna & study
                                   or charity or rituals
                                   or severe austerities

11.49                    don't be miserable
                         don't feel confused
                         cheer up   again
                         be fear free

                         having seen my terrible form
                         see   my form's      this!

11.50   sanjaya to dhrtarashtra : having said so to arjuna  krishna showed his
        human form again nice & mild  let terrified arjuna breathe again

11.51   arjuna:
                        seeing this your gentle human form
                i'm relaxed now my
                mind's back to normal

11.52   krishna: what you've seen   this form
                is hard to get to see
                even the deities want to

11.53           the way you've seen me
                (normally) impossible
                                via vedas or austerity
                                rituals or  charity

11.54           only by single minded devotion
                can i   my truth
                be known  seen
                entered

11.55                                   arjuna
                s/he who

                devoted
                sees me as supreme
                does my work
                        free from
                        attachment & hatred
                        to all beings
                reaches me

12.01     arjuna:

        among

              devotees   always attuned
              who worship your person
                      &
              those who (go for)
              the eternal impersonal
                      who knows yoga better?

12.02     krishna:     those who          mind lost in me
                  worship always attuned

                  blessed with superlative faith
                  they're the most linked  i think  (but)

12.03–04                          those who meditate
                on me    as the
      eternal indeterminate unmanifest omnipresent
        unthinkable fixed immovable constant
              controlling senses
              equable everywhere
              glad in the welfare of all beings

                they too reach me    (though)
12.05     it's harder for them
              attached to the unmanifest  impersonal  (for)

        the unembodied is reached with difficulty by the bodied

12.06–07     offering all work to me supreme
           with single minded yoga   those who
           think of me
           worship me   whose
           thoughts are lost in me

           before long        i uplift them
                      from the ocean
                      of recurring "death"

12.08      put your mind only on me
make your thoughts enter me   you'll
live in me        from now on   there's
       no doubt about that

12.09–10     but if you're incapable of fixing mind on me
practice yoga   to reach me

& if you're no good at that
be keen   do my work

do things for my sake   you'll be
successful

12.11      & if you're powerless to do that too
seek refuge in my power

renounce the results of your actions
& work with self restraint

12.12      better than practice  (of discipline)
is knowledge

better than knowledge
meditation (focus-ability)

& better than that
renunciation
of the fruit of action

12.13–20            s/he who's devoted

       $\&$ friendly  patient  compassionate
       without hatred for all
       free from "this is mine" & "i'm the doer"
       same in happiness & sadness
       always content  self restrained  determined
       mind & thoughts offered to me
       doesn't hate the world  & vice versa
       free from excitement impatience fear distress
       impartial  pure  capable  detached  unanxious
       renouncing all ventures
       doesn't celebrate or hate  mourn or crave
       renounces + & -
       friend = foe  honor = disgrace  praise = blame
       cold = heat  pleasure = pain
       free from attachment  content with anything  silent
       steady  nonmaterialistic

       meditates on this knowledge  nectar
       holds faith
       & is keen
       on me  supreme

    is my love   i repeat!

13.0     arjuna:

     what's prakrti        nature matter energy manifestation

     what's purusa       will spirit person doer

     field  & who knows it

     knowledge        & who knows it

     this  i want to know

13.01      krishna:

         body = field &

         realizer = knower

                 so scholars say

13.02

         in every body

         the knower is me

         so  true knowledge        i believe

         is knowledge of both

                 field & knower

13.03

                 hear from me

                 in summary:

         field: what exactly

         what sort

         how & why it changes

         who's the knower

         & what his powers

13.04

         sung by sages

         in many         well reasoned definitive

         ways

                 hymns  brahmasutras

13.05–06        the field  of change
                is this  in brief

                        the elements   (earth water fire air ether)
                        ego   the "i am the doer" idea
                        intellect
                                including the unmanifest (subconscious)

                        sense apparatus
                        ten + one        (ear eye tongue skin nose
                                          + hands feet mouth anus genital
                                          + mind)
                        sense places
                        five             (sound touch color taste smell)

                        attraction repulsion
                        pleasure pain

                        the organism altogether

                        awareness  will

13.07           & true knowledge
                is this:
                        absence of pride  hypocrisy
                        nonviolence  patience  rightness
                        attention to the teacher
                        self control  purity  constancy

13.08                           keeping
                                birth death aging sickness pain imperfections
                                in mind
                        desirelessness for sense objects
                        "i am the doer" ism

13.09–11                    detachment
            unclinging to home spouse kids etcetera
     levelheadedness
            whatever happens
            whether you like it or not
     unwandering devotion in me  united
     wandering to places of sol
            uncomfortable in crowds
     always aware of the spiritual
            seeing the purpose
            of realization

everything else is
ignorance

13.12                what's got to be known  by which
one gets immortality i'll reveal:
it is brahman
without beginning
the ultimate
neither "is" nor "isn't"

13.13                hand foot eye head face everywhere
ear everywhere
permeating everything

13.14                apparently has the functions  qualities  gunas
of all the senses  but it's
free from all the senses
unattached to anything  yet
holds everything

qualityless yet              has no gunas  but
relishes qualities          experiences through gunas

13.15　　　　　in animate & inanimate
　　　　　　　　　　beings
　　　　　　& out

　　　　　　far away　so close

　　　　　　　　　too subtle to be understood

13.16　　　　　one　not many　　　　　but as if many
　　　　　　parts　　　　　　　　beings

　　　　　　creator
　　　　　　sustainer
　　　　　　devourer　of beings

13.17　　　　　light beyond par
　　　　　　darkness beyond par

　　　　　　knowledge
　　　　　　　　　to be known
　　　　　　　　　　　　goal of knowledge
　　　　　　　　　(right here)
　　　　　　in every
　　　　　　heart

13.18　　　　　in short　field　knowledge　& what's to be known
　　　　　　　　　knowing these my devotee
　　　　　　　　　gets closer to　becomes
　　　　　　　　　me

13.19　　　　　purusa　spirit　person　doer　activator　knower &
　　　　　　prakrti　nature　material field　　　form
　　　　　　　　　　　　　　　　　　　from which rise
　　　　　　　　　　　　　　　　　　　transformations
　　　　　　　　　　　　　　　　　　　& gunas
　　　　　　are both
　　　　　　beginningless

13.20     as for action-reaction-actor
          prakrti's behind it
                    (while)
          purusa
          experiences  causes        (for without purusa there's
          pleasure & pain             no one to experience them)

13.21     purusa
          anchors in nature &
          experiences natureborn gunas

          reborn in wombs            good & bad
          depending on association
          with gunas                 (rebirth depends on
                                     the quality/company
                                     you keep)

13.22     as witness approver
          supporter enjoyer          god
          "ultimate you"             is in this body  as
                                     ultimate purusa

13.23     s/he who knows this        purusa-prakrti-gunas
          no matter where
                    in the lives cycle
          isn't reborn

13.24     some realize themselves    who they really are
          by themselves

          by meditation
          on themselves

          some via samkhya
                    knowledge

          some via karma yoga
                    activity

13.25     others who know no better
          hear about it from others
          & worship it
                    they too cross death
                    devoted to what they've heard of

13.26     whatever is born   arjuna
                    moving  still
          comes from the union
                    of the field & knower

13.27     god is in all beings
          equally
          isn't destroyed when they

                    s/he who can see that
                    has insight

13.28     seeing the same god   god self  everywhere
          doesn't hurt others
                    others = herself

          reaches the ultimate goal

13.29     s/he who realizes that all
          actions are performed by nature
                    & not by the person
          really realizes

13.30     when s/he sees the many states
          rooted on the one   nature
                    branching out from it
          then s/he reaches brahman

13.31          the beginningless featureless
everlasting
ultimate self      ultimate you  god
      although in the body
      doesn't act
      isn't affected

13.32          like ether goes every where
      nothing affects it
the true you  god  in your body
      nothing can touch it

13.33          all it takes is one sun
      the whole world's illuminated
so a knower
      to an entire field

13.34          by knowledge eye  s/he who
differentiates      knower as free from field
      beings as free from matter
s/he goes
to the goal

14.01          i'll say even more
of the best knowledge
by which all seeekers
attain realization

14.02          assured they
got to my state they
are not born at creation
not scared at dissolution

14.03    mighty brahma
is my womb
where i place my seed

the origin of all
beings is
right there arjuna

14.04    for any form from any womb

brahma is womb archetypal womb
i'm dad seed

14.05    sattva – rajas – tamas
are gunas i.e. qualities
natureborn
tie the embodied infinite you
to the body

14.06    sattva:
healthy shining purity
links you to happiness
& knowledge

14.07      rajas:
passion
comes from desire & attachment
links you to action

14.08          tamas comes from ignorance
confuses
links you to confusion
laziness sleepiness

14.09–14.10  when sattva dominates
   → happiness

    when rajas dominates
    → action

     when tamas dominates
     hides knowledge
     → confusion

14.11–13  via all bodygates (nine)
when knowledge light
shines …
… sattva

    greed activity
    stirring lust
    restlessness….
    … rajas

     darkness inertia
     confusion …
     … tamas

14.14–18       when a being with a body
goes through "death"
in the influence
of satva rajas or tamas

sattvic goes stainlessly
to the highest worlds
of knowledgeable

                   rajasic is reborn
                   in the world
                   of action

                             tamasic is reborn
                             in the wombs
                             of the fooled

the result of
sattva action
is pure

                   rajas results in pain
                             tamas in ignorance

from sattva is born
knowledge
           from rajas desire
                 from tamas
                 confusion ignorance

the sattvic goes
up
           rajasic stays in the
           middle
                 tamasic goes
                 below

14.19       when s/he knows
the doer's no other but the gunas
& knows what transcends them
                     s/he attains my state

14.20
        when s/he transcends
these three gunas  that cause the body

s/he's freed
        from birth death age pain
reaches immortality

14.21    arjuna:
        what is the sign of a transcended one
how does s/he behave
how does s/he transcend the three

14.22    krishna:
        in knowledge  activity  confusion
s/he    doesn't hate what's there
        doesn't want what's not

14.23
        s/he who
is as if detached

        by (the three) gunas unperturbed
steady not stirred

        thinks   oh that's them  gunas
        at work

14.24–26
        self reliant  steady   renouncing all ventures
pain = pleasure  stone = gold = clay   loved = not loved
        friend = foe   honor = disgrace  praise = blame

transcends gunas  it is said

14.26        & s/he who          transcending gunas
             with unwandering devotion   bhakti yoga
             serves me
                         is ready
                         to be
                         one
                                     with brahman

14.27                    i am the site
             of brahman of immortal undying eternal law unique bliss

15.01        an endless tree
             the tree of life

             roots above
             limbs below

             & its leaves  they say
             are vedic hymns
                                     s/he who knows this knows the veda

15.02        high & low
             it's branches flow

             qualities feed it

             & objects of desire
             sprout there

             & below
             the stretching (aerial) roots
             plant activities in the world of humans

15.03          you can't quite get it

its form its start its end
& foundation

a full grown root like
this can be cut
only by the strong

with the axe: detachment

15.04               so seek detachment then! there   where
those who go
don't return

(say)      "refuge i seek   in the ancient spirit
that first gushed creativity"

15.05     arrogance
faults &
attachments vanquished

always in the spiritual

turning from lusts
free from pairings   pleasure pain
unfooled   they go
there   the everlasting place

15.06                    unlit by sun
or moon
or fire

it's my place   beyond

they go there   &
don't come back

15.07    a being                      a mere part of me        ancient
         when becoming                in the living world

         draws six senses:
                smell taste touch sight hearing mind

         from matternature
         to itself

15.08    when it   god
         takes a body
         & when it ups & goes

         it carries these (senses) along
         as wind carries scents from a source

                                      (so the spirit carries
                                      its characteristics)

15.09    over hearing sight touch taste smell & mind
         it presides

         & objects of desire
         it savors

15.10    whether it's going or staying or enjoying or if it has qualities
         only the knowing eyes see it
                not the fooled

15.11    striving yogis
         see it in themselves
                the unready don't
                even if they try

15.12     the brilliance     from the sun
                              that illuminates the universe without stop
                in the moon
          in fire
                note  it's mine

15.13      i enter the earth &
          with my energy
          support all beings

          then as soma nectar juicy
          i make all plants blossom

15.14     becoming digestive fire
          i live
          in the body of beings

          with
          inhalation       life breath
          & exhalation     abdominal breath

          i consume        food
          four ways        chew lick
                           swallow suck

15.15     in every heart   i am
          i am memory wisdom & their negation
          i am the author of the vedanta
          the knower of the vedanta

          in the vedas i am
          all that's to be known

15.16    in this world  there are two
         perishable  imperishable

         all beings perish
                 what doesn't change
                 is imperishable

15.17    but there's another  the highest
         the "supreme"

         who enters the three worlds
         & supports them

15.18    because i am beyond the perishable
         because i am beyond the imperishable

         i am    in the world & in the vedas
         known

         as supreme

15.19    s/he who  not a fool
         knows me

                 all-knowing
                 supreme

         adores me
         with her entire
         being

15.20    this supersecret science
         has been spoken by me

         knowing this
         one should become
                 enlightened
                 all duties done

16.01–03        these are the assets
of the inherently divine

        fearless allpure
        set on the way of wisdom
        charitable self controlled & right
        does yagna self study austerities
        nonviolent truthful angerless renunciate
        peaceful notslanderous compassionate
        nondesirous modest gentle unfickle
        radiant patient courageous
        hygienic untreacherous
        not overproud

& these the inherent demonic
        hypocricy egoism
        anger harshness ignorance

16.05        the divine leads to liberation        demonic to bondage

        don't worry
you are born to divine
destiny

16.06        (so) two types of beings in this world
divine
demonic

enough said of the divine
here's more
        about the demonic

16.07

they don't know
when to act
& when to rest

no
purity nicety
truth   in them

16.08

shaky without truth
they say the universe
is godless
one happened without the other

& worse   happened
via lust!

16.09

with this view
these lost smallminded
come up
with terrible acts to
destroy the world

16.10

in desire insatiable
with arrogance hypocrisy
deluded tipsy   they          carry on
hang on to lies &  impure practices

16.11

in infinite worries
unto the end
hedonists
              they're sure that's
              all there is to it

16.12

snared in hundreds of hope ropes
dedicated to anger  desire

they want to make money   in illegal ways
for pleasure

16.13
"this i picked up today
& this heart's desire   i will too
& this is mine    this money
& this too will be mine"

16.14
"that foe's done in   by me
i'll get the others too
i'm god i'm debauchee
successful  powerful  happy"

16.15
"i'm rich i'm classy
no one else compares to me
yeah i'll do the rites  donate  enjoy"

that's how they are    misled
by ignorance
16.16
spun out by many thoughts
netted by delusion
clinging to pleasures
they fall  impure
hell!

16.17
full of themselves  diehards
high & proud on wealth
offer namesake rituals
with hypocrisy
not the correct way

16.18
in a state of egoism power envy
anger desire arrogance   they
hate me in their own
bodies  & others'

16.19
i always throw
these bad cruel haters
the worst of all humans
in this gig
into demonic wombs

16.20

having got there
the fools  birth after birth
not getting to me

they carry on to
worse places

16.21

desire anger greed
are the three gates of hell
one's destruction
one must give them
up

16.22

when free from these three
gates of darkness   arjuna
one does what's good
for oneself &

walks the high way

16.23

s/he who ignores
the scriptures
goes as s/he pleases

reaches neither perfection
nor happiness nor goal

16.24

take the scriptures as your guide
figure out what's to be done
& what not

know what the scriptures say
& do your duty

17.01    arjuna:

what about those
faithful
who chuck out shastras (scriptures rules injunctions)

where do they stand
    sattva   rajas  or tamas

17.02    krishna:    listen

three types of faith
come naturally
for beings  for those in bodies
    sattvic  rajasic  tamasic

17.03

everyone's faith
is in line with her
nature

a person is made of faith
whatever s/he believes
s/he is

17.04

the sattvic offer to deities
the rajasic to spirits & demons
the tamasic to the departed & to ghosts

17.05

those who    not in line with scriptures
do harrowing
penance    with egoism hypocrisy
    passion power desire

17.06

thoughtless torture
of elements    within themselves
    & me

are demonic wills

17.07            besides
the food everyone likes
is three types

different in offering austerity charity

17.08            the sattvic likes
hearty    smooth
                substantial flavor
for truth liveliness strength health
& a happy good feeling

17.09            the rajasic wants
hot        pungent sour salty
                sharp dry
it causes sadness grief illness

17.10            & the tamasic likes
stale        outofflavor
                putrid leftover
                impure rejects

17.11            yagna done correctly  by
those who don't aim at gain
                for offering's sake
                in mind
        = sattvic

17.12            when gain's in view
& the offering's a show
the yagna
= rajasic

17.13            yagna without faith  protocol
                                food  chant
                                gratuity
        = tamasic

17.14     body austerity:
      reverence to deities twiceborn ("castes" 1, 2 and 3)
       teachers & the wise
      purity rightness celibacy nonviolence

17.15     speech austerity:
      words that don't pain
      that are true & nice & mean well
      & holy text repetition

17.16     mind austerity:
      calm gentle silent self controlled
      pure feelings

17.17     this triple discipline
      without agenda
      with high faith
  = sattvic

17.18     when false
      for propriety face ritual
  = rajasic
      unstable shifty

17.19     when it's
with foolish ideas of oneself
      tormented
      or to topple someone
  = tamasic

17.20     a gift that's given
for giving's sake     not to return a favor
      at the right time & place
       to the right person
  = sattvic

17.21   a grudging
       quid pro quo
       for gain
       = rajasic

17.22   at the wrong time & place
       to the wrong person
       with disrespect   contempt
       = tamasic

17.23   *om tat sat*
          set as the
          triple chant of brahman
       organized the priests vedas & yagnas
          way back

17.24   *om*
          the way to start
          a yagna charity
          action austerity
       so say
       the followers of
       brahman   always

17.25   *tat*
       thus

       say those who want
       liberation
          via yagna charity  various
          actions austerity
          not aiming for profit

17.26        *sat*

             i.e.
             in truth
             in goodness

             & said
             for action worth
             appreciating

17.27        when steady in
             sacrifice discipline charity
             said to be *sat*

             related activities
                     said to be *sat*

17.28        austerity activity &
             what's given
             without faith
             is good for nothing        here & hereafter
                     said to be *asat*

18.01    arjuna:
             what's the nature
             of asceticism   i want to know
             how's renunciation
             different

18.02    krishna:
             asceticism is giving up
             selfish activities
                             as poets know
                             & the wise declare
             renunciation is giving up
             fruits of action

18.03        activity's flawed  say the wise
give it up

& others say no
      yagna charity austerity activity
not to be given up

18.04        listen to the last word   mine
on this

three types
of renunciation

18.05                   activity   yagna charity austerity
not to be given up  but rather
to be done

they purify the wise

18.06                   but     my last word
they've got to be done
minus attachment
to fruit of action

18.07        it's not right to give up
activity that's duty

when due to delusion  it's
said to be
tamasic

18.08        when given up
because difficult
because fear of pain  it's
rajasic

no benefit's gained

18.09     when what must be done
        is done disciplined

        giving up attachment gain it's
        sattvic

18.10         doubts snapped off
        the wise one   renunciate
        is full of sattva
           doesn't stick to doing what's nice
             doesn't detest what's not

18.11     it's not possible
        for the one who bears a body
        to give up action entirely

            so
        the one who gives up
           fruit of actions
        is called
        one who gives up renunciate

18.12     those who do not renounce
        have three results
        when they depart
           bad good mixed
        not so
        for those who do

18.13     learn arjuna
           as samkhya philosophy says
        there are five causes
        for the success of all actions

18.14      body     site of action
                   doer     agent
                   organs    instruments
                   activities
                   & divine grace

18.15      whatever one does
                       whether lawful or contrary
                       with body  speech  or mind
                   it's because of these five

18.16             this being so
                   s/he who sees only herself
                   as the doer
                   doesn't get it       in half-baked understanding
                                       the dimwit

18.17      s/he whose attitude
                   not egoistic

                   intellect
                   not unclear

                   even if s/he kills   these people  worlds
                       doesn't really
                   isn't bound

18.18             what's known
                       what's to-be-known
                       & the one who knows
                   cause action

                   & action
                   is made of
                       act
                       actor
                       instrument

18.19          knowledge
action
actor
      according to samkhya
are of three types

18.20         by sattvic knowledge
      one knows one eternal
         in all beings
      unity in diversity

18.21         by rajasic knowledge
      one knows one by one
         many beings

18.22         by tamasic knowledge
      one's attached
      to what's to be done
            pointless  petty
        not why

18.23         sattvic action is
      disciplined
      free from attachment
      without desire hatred
      without wanting gain

18.24         rajasic action is
      selfish
      egoistic
      strenuous

18.25         tamasic action
      started in delusion
      regardless
      of consequence
         harm  loss
      & of one's own (in)competence

18.26   the sattvic doer  is free
           from attachment
      doesn't talk about herself
        steadfast
        enthusiastic
        unchanging
      in success & failure

18.27   the rajasic doer
      passionate  greedy
          wants gain
      by nature violent
      impure
         all joy or grief

18.28   the tamasic doer
      undisciplined deceitful lazy procrastinator
      stubborn depressive wicked show-off

18.29   now for the fine distinctions
   of intelligence
   & will
      as per the gunas  the qualities
   here's a full primer
         hear

18.30   sattvic intelligence understands
   freedom  bondage
   when to act  when not
   what to do  what to fear
   what not

18.31      rajasic intelligence mistakes
      right  with wrong
      what to do   with what not

18.32

tamasic intelligence
steeped in darkness
thinks wrong right
& everything contrary

18.33

a sattvic will
holds     mind  breath of life
& the actions of senses
via yoga   unwavering

18.34

a rajasic will
stays firm
for pleasure  money  righteousness
but selfish
attached

18.35

the tamasic will
stubborn
can't give up
sleep fear grief pride depression
dullhead!

18.36

now hear about happinesses  three
one enjoys   by practice
& goes to
the end of sorrow

18.37

what seems like poison at first
is like nectar   in the end

this happiness  sattvic  said to come
from self insight
& clarity

18.38

the meetings of
senses & objects   seem
like nectar        at first but later
poisonlike         that's rajasic happiness

18.39
                                        tamasic happiness
deludes at first
& in outcome
it comes from
sleep  laziness  negligence

18.40
there isn't one     being   born to matter  nature
on earth or among
the deities in "heaven"
who's free
from these three  gunas  sattvic rajasic tamasic

18.41
the work
of the four "castes"  (brahmin  kshatriya vaisya sudra)
is assigned
by their gunas  their innate nature

18.42
by nature
the work of a brahmin is
peace control austerity purity patience rightness
knowledge wisdom faith

18.43
heroism pageantry will skill
charity grandeur
& not deserting in war
by nature
the work of the kshatriya

18.44
farming shepherding trade
by nature the vaisya's

& by nature
service
the work of the sudra

18.45     when each is delighted in her own
          work reaches perfection

          so hear how   one finds
          perfection in one's own

18.46     by dedicating one's work
          to the
                    origin of beings
                    by whom the universe is permeated
          one reaches perfection

18.47     better to play one's own role   unremarkable
          than another's role well

          working in line with innate nature
          one isn't culpable

18.48     mustn't give up
          work you're born with
                    even when it's not nice
          (& anyway) all missions are clouded by flaws
                    as fire  by smoke

18.49     one achieves
          ideal actionlessness  by
                    renunciation
                    self mastery
                    desirelessness
                              & an always detached
                    intelligence

18.50     after perfection how
          does one attain brahman
                    the highest state
                              knowledge
          here's a brief

18.51–53      by pure intelligence  attuned
determined controlled
        giving up egoism aggression arrogance desire
        anger possessiveness attraction repulsion sound &
        other sense objects
        living alone eating lightly
        controlling speech mind body
        relying on detachment
        peaceful  unselfish
        always in yoga  the highest
one gets fit
for        oneness with
brahman

18.54      one with brahman
soothed        neither mourns nor wants
to all beings   equal
to me   most devoted

18.55      through devotion
aware        who i am
        what i am
      & knowing my reality
        at once enters me

18.56      relying on me
for all work always
s/he reaches      by my grace
eternal infinite place

18.57      mentally   give it all up
        over to me   supreme
take refuge in wisdom as yoga
        mind on me   constantly be

18.58      you'll cross the hard times by my grace
but if  egoistic you
don't listen  you're
finished

18.59          if you think
               "i'm-the-doer  so
               i won't fight"
          your idea's in vain  for
          your nature will push you

18.60          you're bound to your duty  your destiny
          by your innate nature

          what you don't wish
          to do you will
          do against your will
          in delusion

18.61          god lives in the heart of all beings
          & by maya   power  illusion
          makes them move  as if
               strung on a gizmo

18.62          go to god  only
          with your entire being
          from that grace  you'll find
          a most peaceful place  forever

18.63          thus

          knowledge
          secret of secrets
          has been explained to you

          think it over
          all of it

          then do as you wish

18.64     & most secret of all  again
                    my last word
          listen  again

          you are loved   for sure
          by me

          so i'll speak
          for your good

18.65     heart be full of me
          be devoted to me
          do the rites for me
          do homage to me  you'll

          come to me
          i promise    truly
          you are
          my love

18.66     give up    your given duties
          trust me only

          i'll free you from all sins
                    don't worry

18.67                              this (*gita*)   must not be told
                                   to one without austerity  faith
                                   who doesn't want to hear it
                                   & who speaks ill of me

18.68                              s/he who lays out
                                   this utter secret
                                   to my devotees
                                        the highest act of devotion
                                   will come to me  without doubt

18.69
& no one
does more loving
service  than her

& no one
will be more beloved
to me  than her

18.70
s/he who studies this
nice dialog of ours

i'll be loved
by her knowledge-yagna
that's my take

18.71
even s/he who merely hears it
full of faith  uncynical
is freed
& goes to happy worlds
of those with pure actions

18.72
has all this
been heard by you   arjuna
with a focused mind

has your ignorance & confusion
been destroyed

18.73     arjuna:
lost delusion
gained wisdom  memory
by your grace   o unchanging krishna

i stand corrected  doubts gone
i will do as you say

Mani Rao

18.74    sanjaya:

this
wonderful dialog
          krishna & arjuna's
is what i heard

so rare  it makes
one's hair stand on end

18.75                                  by the grace of vyasa    (author of mahabharata
                                                                                          in which   the *gita*)
i've heard this utter secret
which krishna himself
said

18.76    king dhrtarashtra
              again & again i
                      remember this
              holy  wonderful dialog
              between krishna & arjuna

again & again
i feel happy

18.77                                  again & again i
              remember krishna's very wonderful form
              & again & again
              i feel happy
                      o king my
                      astonishment is great

18.78        i believe
wherever there is krishna  the master of yoga
wherever there is arjuna  the archer
there will be

beauty
victory
prosperity

steady righteousness